Out Of
SYLLABUS

Career Success Tips that no one taught You

V. Rajesh

Published by:

V&S PUBLISHERS

F-2/16, Ansari road, Daryaganj, New Delhi-110002
☎ 011-23240026, 011-23240027 • *Fax:* 011-23240028
Email: info@vspublishers.com • *Website:* www.vspublishers.com

Branch: Hyderabad
5-1-707/1, Brij Bhawan (Beside Central Bank of India Lane)
Bank Street, Koti Hyderabad - 500 095
☎ 040-24737290
E-mail: vspublishershyd@gmail.com

Distributors:

▶ **Pustak Mahal®**
J-3/16, Daryaganj, New Delhi-110002
☎ 011-23276539, 011-23272783, 011-23272784 • *Fax:* 011-23260518
E-mail: sales@pustakmahal.com • *Website:* www.pustakmahal.com
Bengaluru: ☎ 080-22234025 • *Telefax:* 080-22240209
Patna: ☎ 0612-3294193 • *Telefax:* 0612-2302719

▶ **PM Publications**
- 10-B, Netaji Subhash Marg, Daryaganj, New Delhi-110002
  ☎ 011-23268292, 011-23268293, 011-23279900 • *Fax:* 011-23280567
  E-mail: pmpublications@gmail.com
- 6686, Khari Baoli, Delhi-110006
  ☎ 011-23944314, 011-23911979

▶ **Unicorn Books**
23-25, Zaoba Wadi (Opp. VIP Showroom), Thakurdwar, Mumbai-400002
☎ 022-22010941 • *Telefax:* 022-22053387

© **Copyright: Author**
ISBN 978-93-815882-7-7
Edition : 2012

The Copyright of this book, as well as all matter contained herein (including illustrations) rests with the Publisher. No person shall copy the name of the book, its title design, matter and illustrations in any form and in any language, totally or partially or in any form. Anybody doing so shall face legal action and will be responsible for damages.

Printed at : Param Offset Okhla, New Delhi

Dedication

This book is dedicated to all my mentors, well-wishers and Gurus I have been lucky to have had. I hope that the inputs, I have had, which are captured in this book help enrich the lives of the reader as it has mine.

Publisher's Note

"Your book bag has transformed into a brief case and your casual attire into business attire; it's time to start thinking like a professional."

Making the transition from College/ University Campus to Corporate World is one of the biggest challenges students face in their career as they confront an inevitable transition from the happy assignments and mid-semesters scenario to team work and deadlines. Moving from an academic environment to a corporate setting has many changes and one needs to understand the organisational dynamics in order to get well in this new environment as corporate houses prefer to recruit employees who can be immediately employed and deployed.

Training college/ university students to make them more employable is one of the key challenges for most of the companies across the world. So it is evident that companies also feel the necessity to groom the fresh students to make them more professional and fitted to a corporate setup and that is why companies organise various workshops to groom their employees. However, in most of the cases it is seen that these workshops end in incomplete training and disappointment.

Students and youngsters find it difficult to adapt the requirements of corporate environment primarily because of the vast difference in the way professors and managers operate; while professors focus on increasing learning quotient and improving subject matter understanding, managers want implementation of the knowledge and therefore focus on getting the task done, meeting deadlines, etc. So, while one focuses on learning, the other focuses on significant leverage. This added pressure takes a heavy toll on students and makes it even more difficult for them to scale the success ladder at corporate level. Besides handling these pressures, it is becoming more and more important to have the correct know-how to proceed in career.

To bridge the gap that exists between Campus environment and Corporate setting and to help those students who are just entering the Corporate World or in the threshold of Campus and Corporate, **V&S Publishers** launches its imprint – **Campus to Corporate.**

Foreword

The Syllabus is a pivotal thing in the formative years of anyone. Our lives are defined by the syllabus. Even when not finished on time it causes serious concern and angst in the minds of students as this typically leads to special classes, Saturday school, etc. Before any test or exam we are all worried only about the portions from the syllabus that are included for that test or exam. Most things we don't know conveniently become out of syllabus for the exam and hence the responsibility no longer rests on the student's shoulders.

Overnight, this mighty thing called as syllabus becomes powerless.

A common quotation is "Just when I learnt all the answers to life, the questions changed". In other words, this means that the syllabus followed till then was no longer relevant. One can leave a question during an exam and expect full marks for that if the question happens to be out of syllabus. But in real life, there is nothing called as "Out of Syllabus". Especially when a person embarks on his career this excuse of "out of syllabus" becomes unacceptable.

In that context the various syllabus taught to us during the 17 plus long years of study which is filled with many things should ideally prepare us completely at least for a career and especially success in one's career, if not to handle life.

Unfortunately, that is not the case. Success is not wholly based on pure academic knowledge. Actually what students get during their 17 plus long years of study is academic information, not knowledge, and this difference between information and knowledge is one of the many things this book will explain. There is obviously a huge gap with regard to various inputs required to be successful in a career. Sadly, this is not taught to the vast majority during the almost 2 decades of academic preparation towards a career.

These crucial inputs end up being "Out of Syllabus".

As mentioned before, in the tests of daily life one cannot escape by using the excuse of "Out of Syllabus". That is why most people are handicapped when managing their careers and this leads to frustrations, stress and unhappiness. And obviously is nowhere near success.

One interesting reality is that many if not most successful and visionary people are those who chose to spend time to learn the lessons which are "Out of Syllabus". In fact there are many examples of people dropping out of formal education and being phenomenally successful, mainly because of their "Out of Syllabus" learning.

However, everyone who drops out of formal education cannot be assured of success by default. A conscious awareness is required that life will cast situations which are "Out of Syllabus" and efforts to learn about handling the same will definitely increase the chances of success.

This book *Out of Syllabus* covers those inputs, tips, guidelines and suggestions that are hardly ever taught formally to anyone. A few lucky people might get to

FOREWORD

learn some of these things from their parents, friends, colleagues, etc. But most are bereft of these crucial inputs. These "Out of Syllabus" lessons will help a person become more effective and efficient and also leverage his academic learning in a better manner.

One very interesting and important concept discussed in the book is about "Personal Success Secret". This is one of the bedrocks of success and if you look around and notice any successful person you will find that they have their own "Personal Success Secrets".

The inputs discussed in the book are very basic and simple and are not rocket science. The key to making it work is to internalise these inputs and make them into habits through repetitive learning as the author often mentions.

The author's intent to help enrich the lives of the reader is surely possible because of the simplicity of the ideas and the ease with which it can be incorporated into one's life. We do hope that you derive the maximum benefits from this book and also share the learning with others to enrich the lives of others around you.

True success lies in being remembered as a great human being who made a difference in the lives of others. Hope every reader achieves this success.

Contents

I.	Introduction & Overview	13
II.	Importance of Career Planning	18
III.	The Three Bucket Theory of Career Planning	22
IV.	**The 1st Bucket**	**26**
	❑ Life skills learning	30
	❑ Functional learning	36
	❑ Organisational learning	38
	❑ Personal effectiveness	40
V.	**The 2nd Bucket**	**44**
	❑ Defining your Personal Success Secret	50
	❑ Developing Behaviours for Success	57
	○ Harmony and Balance	58
	○ Urgent Vs Important	61
	○ How is it relevant?	66
	○ Learning never stops	70
VI.	**The 3rd Bucket**	**74**
	❑ Confidence Vs Overconfidence	75

❏	What is the "Wallenda Factor" and how to avoid it	77
❏	People first	81

VII. The most important one; The 4th Bucket!   **86**

VIII. The Last Word   **90**

Introduction & Overview

There is a common saying in corporate circles which is "What is measured can be managed". The unsaid part of this statement is that one needs to plan and set definitive objectives and only then can anything be measured. So it is with one's career. Usually one's career is supposedly planned because everyone tends to study based on this plan and aspirations. However, most often this is not well thought out and the criteria used for career planning is misguided to say the least.

The criteria to decide on careers vary from personal choice (rarely) to parental pressures, peer group influence, monetary considerations, etc. The issue is that these factors very soon lose relevance and a person is left wondering about the career (s)he is pursuing. By then time has also passed by and people tend to get by in this default choice of a career. Considering this, is it any wonder that the stress from job related issues is on the rise and most people don't seem to be happy?

This fundamental flaw in career planning is best illustrated by this incident I once witnessed. A lady with her daughter had come for counselling. This lady was lamenting that her daughter used to be a very good student and was consistently topping the class in her school. The previous year they managed to get her a seat in one of the best engineering colleges and that's when the trouble started. The daughter had progressively become dull, morose and lost interest in everything including studies. Obviously she was doing very poorly in the college and this was becoming a major cause of concern. It was then the turn of the daughter to express her views.

The daughter started off being withdrawn. But, with gentle prodding started opening up and said that she did like the college and the students there. She had no problem with anyone there. After a few repeated questions about what was the reason for her dullness and poor performance, she suddenly burst out, "I don't want to be an engineer. I don't want to study engineering." A second of silence followed.

Then her mother very forcefully and almost curtly told her daughter, "You don't know. You want to be an engineer. You study well and can become a good engineer and earn lots of money."

This incident sadly reflects how the career choices for youngsters are made.

I cannot claim to have been blessed with foresight and had planned my career with perfection. However, what I can claim is that several mentors and well-wishers gave me very good and sound advice which I internalised and acted upon. Over the years this has helped me shape my career broadly in the way I would have liked it to be. I firmly believe that there is no single success formula and in that context am very sceptical of self-improvement books such as this one itself.

Therefore, what I put forward through this book is to be taken as an indicative direction and as inputs which

INTRODUCTION & OVERVIEW

need to be thought about and then one needs to structure these ideas and inputs to suit his self, his personality, his aspirations, etc. If these inputs are well adapted and acted upon, they will develop into your own unique success formula which is not only powerful but also enduring.

Lastly, nothing is static and unchangeable. The environment changes, we change, our expectations change. In this ever evolving scenario, your plan should also be flexible to adapt itself to these changes to be a lasting success. This is the most difficult part because we are very afraid to let go of something which seems to be successful. By the time it stops being effective and we realise that change is needed, it is usually late.

This book is a compilation of several such wonderful advices which I have acted upon and is therefore tried and tested. The book also details several live instances which will help one to understand the point being made and make it easy to internalise.

The book elaborates and details a theory about career planning and achieving success in one's career. A basic idea of this theory was told to me by a well-wisher many years ago. Over the years many of my other well-wishers and mentors have given me inputs at various points in my career which have been very relevant and more importantly effective. I have built upon this basic idea, adding on all these inputs to the relevant phases of one's career to develop this into an actionable theory for career success. I confidently state that this is actionable as I have actively implemented it as much as possible. Also, when I see the career paths of several successful people, the theme is broadly the same and can very much be identified with this theory. I am sure that readers who understand these inputs and adapt it to their life can also make it work and get great benefits.

The book also delves into the concept of success formulas and tries to come up with a method of Personal Success for an individual (what exactly is one for any individual). This is crucial as everyone is seeking success and understanding this method will greatly enhance the chances of personal success. Obviously, success is dependent on not only some actions but also some behaviours which ensure that one's perception and management of situations has a greater chance of success.

These behaviours need to be consciously developed and practised to ensure that they get ingrained in a person and therefore the response to any situation is defined by these ingrained thinking and behavioural patterns.

There are many people that I see and meet who are fairly successful in their career or professional life; however, not very happy in their personal life. I have seen executives earning very well get into serious financial problems as also very popular managers whose team adore them but have severe issues with their personal relationships. This is because of a simple mind block and this is discussed towards the end of this book.

Last but not the least is the section which helps a person to leap from being 'good' and 'great' to 'outstanding' by using the power of faith. There is an increasing body of evidence which details out how prayer is helpful in

INTRODUCTION & OVERVIEW

achieving so many things. There are recorded instances of people overcoming illnesses thanks to prayer. What is this power and how can this be harnessed to achieve career success and personal happiness? The details are covered in the last chapter.

Lastly I would like to quote Mr Albert Schweitzer. He said: "Success is not the key to happiness. Happiness is the key to success." A simple but profound statement. This is echoed in an another saying which goes like this – "Do what you like and you will never have to work a single day of your life."

How are you going to take the inputs in this book and translate it into your personal success and happiness?

First, read the book slowly. Stopping often to think about the highlighted points in the boxes and relating it to yourself, your aspirations and your plans. Then, let the thoughts from the book be in your mind while you think about your current scenario while these ideas get slowly internalised. Lastly, get a paper and pen out and start putting your plan for a career and success. Most importantly, pursue this with great commitment and belief. This can be done by anyone at any point of time in their career and life. Because, tomorrow when you wake up it will be the first day of the rest of your wonderful and unique life.

Importance of Career Planning

A career as defined by the Oxford dictionary in the noun form is "an occupation undertaken for a significant period of a person's life and with opportunities for progress". The origin of this word is supposed to date back to the 16th century and is derived from the French word carrière, from Italian word carriera, which in turn is based on Latin carrus 'wheeled vehicle'. So, the original reference for this word was race related.

Hence the unstated association with competition, victory, etc., as also the oft mentioned rat race!

Ironically the same Oxford dictionary has a different meaning for the word career when used in a verb form. It means "move swiftly and in an uncontrolled way".

Before moving on let us be clear about the concept of noun and verb because it has a lot of relevance to what is being written about in the book.

Noun is a word used to identify any of a class of people, places, or things, or to name a particular one of these.

Verb is a word used to describe an action, state, or occurrence

So, when career is used as a noun to describe anyone's occupation, it is positive and relates to the person's life, progress, etc. However, the same word when used as a verb denotes lack of control and therefore chaos.

IMPORTANCE OF CAREER PLANNING

This difference in meaning is very apt because this is exactly what happens in most cases. Careers are ideally to be planned and acted upon to enable progress over a person's lifetime. However, most often, it ends up being chaotic and uncontrolled because people act (verb orientation) without thinking or planning.

In many of the developed countries where basic needs are not a major worry and there are adequate avenues for anyone to explore his areas of interest, career becomes a fairly planned thing which is oriented towards overall progress and growth.

Unfortunately, that is not the case with the majority in India. In India, career is seen as a means to an end of monetary and materialistic benefits instead of being an end by itself. This means that every possible opportunity or even perceived opportunity is grabbed with both the hands and there is very little if any of planning.

Given the social patterns in India and the influences of the family, friends and peer groups, the career orientation is defined more by pleasing others or living up to someone else's expectation.

Finally the post-liberalisation boom has led to a skewed expectation from a career focusing more on monetary and materialistic returns from day one.

When I decided to join the Retail industry in the mid 90's when there was nothing called as corporate retail, I faced an uphill task. Most of my friends and relatives were worried or even scornful about my intention to be a part of creating an industry and redefining customer preferences and habits. The standard phrase I heard was that "You are crazy. Who will come and shop at supermarkets? Very soon you will be searching for another job and then remember I warned you."

Most if not every youngster faces similar pressures when crafting their careers. The pressure is either to keep up the family name, earn more, match up to relatives, etc., etc.

The core reality to all that has been mentioned till now is the crucial and critical need to plan one's career. Obviously, there should be inputs from various quadrants and stakeholders, but everyone should realise that the career is theirs and therefore the plan has to be their own.

It is relevant to mention the story of the great sage Valmiki who is believed to have authored the Indian epic, *Ramayana*. He was a ruthless bandit and justified his choice of vocation, if one may call it that, by convincing himself that his family needs him to provide for several things and therefore he was correct in being a bandit. One day he came across a sage and the sage asked him whether his family will

It is your life and your career. Expecting someone else to plan and steer it towards success is nothing but emotional and intellectual laziness.

share in the sins being accumulated by Valmiki by being a bandit. He went back and asked his family and was rudely shocked when they said no, they would not share his sins.

IMPORTANCE OF CAREER PLANNING

Similarly, you should remember that they alone will enjoy the fruits of their career choices be it good or bad. Ask anyone who is thrusting their advice regarding careers if they will share the pains and tribulations of a career and the answer will be a resounding NO.

If that be the case, the onus of planning for preparing for one's career clearly falls on the individual and at best others can provide only inputs.

I am sure that by now the importance of planning out one's career choices, path and defining a blueprint for the same is amply clear to the reader.

Very simply put, if you do not know where you want to go, anything can become the destination and that might not be acceptable.

The Three Bucket Theory of Career Planning

Times are changing and so are expectations. There used to be a scenario when people would book a scooter in India and then wait for even many years to get the same. Today, everything is expected instantly. Instant noodles to instant recreation to the expectation of instant gratification. But, wait a minute. Can this instant concept also be extended into one's career?

I very much doubt it.

Of course, the time periods can be crunched which is why there is a craze for management education and degrees. The unsaid expectation is that such an education or at least a degree is a guarantee to fast track career success. Is that possible?

To an extent, it is possible. But not in isolation. A degree is just like a visa stamp. It enables one to enter the domain of management at relatively higher level. However, just like how a visa is only a stamp and what a person is able to do in the country he/she goes to is dependent on the person, so is the case with any degree, especially a management degree. The fact that some of the leaders in business have actually dropped out of such courses is proof enough that it is the individual and his capability that truly matters.

It also helps if the person works smarter and not only harder. The old saying that success does not have any shortcuts is only partially true nowadays. Sustainable success can be achieved by any individual by working smartly instead of only working hard.

Working smartly starts with planning and thinking ahead. A career for many people is something that happens almost by default. This is because the motivations, objectives and therefore the plan for their career are not very clear as also keep changing a lot. Although flexibility is required given the constantly changing environment and context, some basic goal posts cannot shift all the time.

One of the most effective inputs I have ever received about career planning is to look at it in a modular manner. This helps in various ways –

- It takes into account the stage a person is in his/her life.
- It also includes what typically any organisation would expect of an individual as also what they would be ready to give to that person in return.
- It factors in the cascading effect of our actions that over a period of time helps or hinders our progress.

- Most importantly it gives anyone a long term, medium term and immediate perspective and actionable goals to work towards.

I can personally vouch that this modular approach works and I have advocated this concept in several forums and amongst audiences of different age groups and backgrounds. The majority have reverted with a very positive feedback especially that this concept has helped clearly define the steps required to reach their ultimate goals.

Contrarily, some youngsters have also challenged this concept saying that this does not cater to the instant gratification expectation.

My counter to that is that this theory is based on a modular fashion to actually cater to the instant gratification mind-set simply because one needs to expect different things during the three different modules of career progression.

I call this as the "3 Bucket Theory of Career Success" and a broad idea about this was shared with me during a brief interaction many years ago. Over the years, I have not only worked hard to follow this approach but have also consciously taken note of my experiences during these phases of my career. This has enabled me to structure this basic idea into a sound and actionable theory which can be confidently validated by my personal experience.

This book is written with the anticipation that the "3 Bucket Theory of Career Success" helps many people to structure their careers better and become more successful by smart application of this theory.

THE THREE BUCKET THEORY OF CAREER PLANNING

A typical career used to span three decades plus. However, nowadays this has shrunk and the career spans a wide range of time periods. This also includes the reality that several people today explore a mid-life career shift and start off on a whole new line of work. Regardless, anyone's career span can be split into three broad sections. These are what I call buckets and I shall explain why.

In each of these buckets, the person's focus should be on filling the bucket with one specific thing. This gives the person tremendous focus and also provides immediate gratification and satisfaction when they see the results of their efforts filling the bucket.

The 1st Bucket

Typically the first bucket coincides with the early years of anyone's career. Although everyone is armed with an appropriate degree and loads of conceptual inputs and learnings, what is lacking is transformation of that information to knowledge. In addition to this there exist several areas of learning gap which is not addressed in most educational institutes. Referred to as life skills, these are some essentials skills for survival, being effective and growth.

First let us understand the difference between information and knowledge because unless one does so, they will not be able to correctly evaluate whether what they possess is knowledge or mere information.

Let me explain this with a personal anecdote. Years ago I used to work for a multinational soft drinks company. The unsaid rule of that company was that everyone should go "route riding" at periodic intervals. Route riding is not as exotic as it sounds. This is the practise of accompanying a salesman and the designated delivery truck for an entire day while they work in the market and visit every store to take back the empty bottles and sell them crates of the filled ones.

I had joined them as an executive in the marketing department and was promptly despatched for the mandatory

THE 1ST BUCKET

route riding experience. There I was riding in the truck talking to the route agent and the salesman bringing into the picture all the nice things I had learnt in my management course. Obviously, the topic of customer satisfaction and how to handle customer issues came up and I could see the others give me polite smiles when I espoused all that I had learnt in my various classes. After stopping at a few smaller shops and observing the way the transactions were being done, we stopped at a fairly large store. There was a crowd of people purchasing various things and we waited for the owner to get some breathing space to interact with him.

Finally the owner was relatively free and turned towards our group and his face immediately frowned. He literally barked out at the route agent and the salesperson, "Now what? Why have you come?"

The salesman promptly pushed me forward and introduced me as a marketing person. I felt very nice and also important. Putting on my best smile and what I thought was the appropriate corporate expression, smiled and asked the mandatory "how are you?"

In hindsight, it might have been better for me to keep my mouth shut. Better still, if I had not gone to that shop at all. Because, the shop owner scowled at me and shouted, how he would be a lot better if not for the company I worked for and the sales guy and the route agent. At least then I should have kept quiet. But, then all the classes of sales management and handling difficult customers flooded into my mind and I decided to seize this opportunity to show how well I could handle the situation and prove to everyone my managerial capability.

So, I opened the floodgates by asking what the problem was and how I could help. The shop owner bluntly said that I could help by giving a few crates of soft drinks free of cost and that would solve the problem. After hearing this, I was at a complete loss and just stared at everyone standing around me. I did not know the background or the reason for this demand and definitely did not have the authority to do what the shop owner asked for. Thankfully, the sales person stepped in and I guess he must have thought that I had suffered enough.

He tried placating the shop owner and saying that the matter was being resolved. From the ongoing debate I could figure out that the dispute was relating to some sales promotion offer and the shop owner felt that he was due some free crates of soft drink. And this was not shared by the sales person. Unwittingly I had stepped into the middle of this dispute by trying to an the important marketing person.

Soon, it was obvious that the shop owner was in no mood to let the matter rest and let us go. He then turned to me and asked me if I could do something about this. To which I promptly said that I would speak to the sales manager when I get back. The unsaid plea being, please let us escape!

But that was not to be.

The shop owner promptly pulled out the landline phone from under his cash counter, dialled the office number and thrust it at me saying "you can speak to the sales manager now itself." Again, I was caught. So asked the receptionist to connect me to the sales manager.

The receptionist said that the sales manager was in a review meeting and cannot be disturbed. In my best apologetic tone I told this to the shop owner. The shop

THE 1ST BUCKET

owner grabbed the phone and told the receptionist a simple and eternal truth which is hardly ever taught in any institute.

He said: "Call the manager. If we don't stand in the heat and dust to sell your products, you will not be able to conduct any meeting at all in the air conditioned rooms". Needless to say, the sales manager was called and the matter resolved.

That day, I realised how little I knew and how much more I need to learn. That thought has never left my mind and even today consciously try to learn something every day from every situation I am faced with.

There are many things I learnt from this incident. However, the most important and relevant to this book was to learn to be open to learning.

This incident also made me realise and appreciate the difference among information, knowledge and wisdom. I went into this situation with lots of information gathered from my academic learning. Most of this information was relevant and apt. However, only after I experienced this

> Information by itself is only data and is useless. To transfer it to knowledge, one should understand the applicability, context and consequences. Then it becomes actionable and therefore has value.

situation did I learn the context and how to apply and use that information for it to be effective and produce results. That's why I feel that this incident helped open my eyes about the difference between information and knowledge.

Information is data. It is useless by itself, unless acted upon. Most importantly, it creates a false sense of knowing things and many a times blinds us to the learning opportunity because we think that we know it all, already.

Learning, learning and more learning should be the core focus and objective of anyone's 1st bucket towards creating a successful career. Again, here I reiterate, learning should be from a knowledge perspective and not just gathering more information.

Keep an open mind and learn from everything and everyone around you. This sounds simple and obvious, yet it is not so. In fact I think this is the most difficult bucket of anyone's career and unless one is very clear and focussed approaching this, the chances of getting lost is very high. Learning during this stage can be broadly categorised into the following groups:

Life skills learning

These are very basic and can sometimes even seem to be silly. Life skills are typically those skills that are required to handle the problems or issues encountered in day-to-day life. They are crucial to survive and without survival, obviously there is no success. Most of the life skills are built upon common sense and logic. However, a person needs to invest time and effort in learning the nuances of applying common sense and logic to that particular life skill. Unfortunately these skills are rarely included in any formal educational system and unless one consciously works towards learning and developing them, they will be handicapped.

Life skills enable one to enhance the effectiveness of the functional and professional knowledge by being able to be more effective and efficient.

A simple example is to be able to read maps. In India, reading maps for finding a destination might seem silly, even irrelevant, when one can stop anywhere and get directions from someone. Imagine if you are sent abroad for some work and stopping at the roadside for directions is no longer an option. What will you do? Similarly, using a library or conducting a search or research regarding any topic is a basic skill. Even with the most efficient and advanced search engines, this requires some skill because one needs to know the combination of words to use for the search. Imagine a situation when you are entrusted with a task of getting detailed information about something and you kept going back to your superior to get inputs on how to complete this task. Will this reflect very well on your capability?

The World Health Organisation (WHO) has defined ten essential life skills and they are:

1. Self-awareness
2. Empathy

3. Critical thinking
4. Creative thinking
5. Decision making
6. Problem Solving
7. Effective communication
8. Interpersonal relationship
9. Coping with stress
10. Coping with emotion

A brief explanation for each of these life skills is as follows –

★ **Self-awareness:** This is nothing but being aware of our self, independent of the situation and in an objective manner. Usually, we get conditioned to linking our self-image to that of the external context. When receive praise we think that we are great and vice versa. Self-awareness is an objective evaluation of one's strength and more importantly the weaknesses. In fact understanding our weaknesses is as important if not more than knowing our strengths.

★ **Empathy:** This is the capability to truly put yourself in the shoes of an another person and then reacting to a situation. This is very much different from sympathy. Sympathy is when you try to understand another person's situation from your point of view. Learning the art of empathising is a crucial element in becoming a great leader.

★ **Critical thinking:** This is the skill to be able to think about any situation or context in an objective and independent manner without being influenced by how it is being presented, who presents it, etc. Again, it's an important skill to become great leaders as anyone would not like to follow someone who is easily influenced by others.

- **Creative thinking**: What one sees more often is linear thinking, where the thinking is in a sequence and goes from point A to Point B and so on. Creative thinking is not about art and painting in this context. This refers to the skill that enables a person to think in a holistic manner and therefore be able to come up with "out of the box" solutions. This skill is an important component of personal success. Linear thinkers will follow the path that most people do while creative thinkers are those who usually find the shortcut that gets them ahead, faster and with lesser effort.

- **Decision making**: Decision making is not about making decisions only. It is about learning to make the right decisions using several other life skills, at the right time and acting upon the same for the decision to be effective and meaningful.

- **Problem solving**: This is a very crucial skill and closely linked to creative thinking. Unfortunately, most of us consider problem solving to be limited to the maths class of our school days. In reality problem solving is the skill to be able to evaluate a problem and select the best solution, decide on the course of action and act upon it. The core to problem solving lies in the ability to come up with several solutions, many of which should be "out of the box".

- **Effective communication**: We often say to someone else "You have not understood what I said". This in effect means that the person saying this has not learnt the art of effective communications. Any communication is effective only when the recipient of the same understands it as intended by the person communicating. Therefore the responsibility of making one's communication understandable falls on the sender and not the receiver. This involves learning to communicate the Right thing at the Right time to the Right person in the Right way to ensure that they response in the Right manner.

★ **Interpersonal relationships**: This refers to the skill that enables a person to build and sustain a meaningful relationship with others. The focus is on the word 'meaningful'; wherein all parties involved in the relationship should find it meaningful. This is an important skill in the context of team building and management. Unless others who are in a relationship with you find it meaningful the relationship will not sustain and therefore cannot lead to anything positive.

★ **Coping with stress**: This is yet another very important life skill. In today's fast pace of life, everyone is exposed to stress regardless of age or gender. The important factor here is that most people don't realise that stress is something they cause to themselves. Because of this, they blame external factors and others and search for its solutions outside. To be able to handle stress successfully one needs to be self-aware and more importantly choose their response. A simple method of handling stress is to do breathing exercises and/ or meditation. Very simply, this slows down your emotional response and thereby gives you a clearer perspective of the situation thereby enabling you to decide on an appropriate response instead of getting stressed. Here again, other life skills – problem solving and decision making are required; only breathing exercises or meditation will not do.

- **Coping with emotion**: This is possibly the most misunderstood and confusing life skill. Coping with emotion does not mean suppressing the same as this will only lead to stress. Neither does it mean bursting out in joy, anger or despair as this might end up being counterproductive. Coping with emotions is also not limited to coping with one's own emotions but includes coping with others' emotions also. Emotions are volatile and when they are running high people act without thinking. So, this becomes essential in the context of being able to handle any situation.

By now you would have realised how each of these life skills leads into another and is interdependent for it to be effective. Therefore, only one will not be enough and a person needs to learn and master all these life skills. Although in recent times some of these have been included in the syllabus of certain educational organisations, this is hardly taught in a comprehensive manner. These actually cannot be taught inside a classroom. These skills are experiential based and the learning is completely dependent on individuals and what they perceive of the experience.

Look back and think whether you were taught all these skills in your college/ universities or have you ever worked towards learning and honing the same? My guess would be that your answer will be NO.

So in the 1st Bucket the most important thing to fill your bucket is these life skills. These need to be learned and accumulated through your experiences, by observing others, actively seeking inputs and guidance, etc. Suffice to say that this learning itself will keep a person busy enough for quite some time.

Functional learning

The concepts that we study during the period of our formal education provide us with a basic understanding of the subject. At best it gives everyone a good understanding about the subject. However, if anyone thinks that these concepts can be taken and implemented without understanding the practical applicability, they are sorely mistaken. In the movie "Matrix" one of the characters wants to fly a helicopter. The required data is uploaded to her brain and she starts flying the helicopter like an expert. This happens only in movies!

Would you allow someone to conduct an experiment on you just because he/she has read a book about that? Would you agree to get on an aeroplane which is being flown by someone who has just finished learning how to fly an aeroplane only on computer software?

If your answer is no, then why should any organisation allow anyone to independently handle any functional activity just because he has read about that subject. This is the reason why many of the business schools nowadays are increasingly insisting that only persons with some work experience can join the course. This ensures that they understand the subjects better from a practical perspective and more importantly they can be given important responsibilities when they join any organisation after passing out.

THE 1ST BUCKET

> What is learnt at educational institutes is second hand and also does not cover the entire universe. As such a degree is not a guarantee for knowing everything.

Therefore this is the next important thing to fill in the 1st Bucket. One should leave aside unrealistic expectations, ego-based issues and focus on learning the practical aspects of the functions that he/she studied. One should understand that reading and studying something only creates a basis for better understanding.

To be able to truly learn the practical aspects of any function, one should be willing and eager to roll up his sleeves and dirty his hands. There is nothing wrong in doing the most basic jobs in any particular area and this does not lower anyone's worth. In fact, the reality is that such exposure actually increases the professional worth of anyone. You would have read about so many entrepreneurs who have even dropped out of college and yet become very successful. However, you will never come across someone who can achieve success without getting down and griming his hands with work.

There is a valid reason why many feel that doing certain things is beneath their dignity and look down upon such work. This happens when someone is not taught about the concept of "Dignity of Labour". Dignity of labour means that everything and anything done by anyone has a value and should be given due respect. When people start following the concept of "Dignity of Labour", the person doing the task feels proud of whatever is being done. When the society looks down on certain kinds of work, it is obvious that people doing such work are looked down upon and therefore their labour does not enjoy the deserving dignity. The best way to explain this concept is by quoting a scene from the Hindi film "Munnabhai MBBS", where the hero, Sanjay Dutt, hugs a janitor and explains to him how important the job of cleaning floors is. Suddenly, the janitor discovers a new pride in the work he has been doing.

Organisational learning

Every institution or organisation operates in a different manner depending on their core activities and the type of people who are the majority. In educational institutions, the operating style is very different from corporates. Educational institutes operate with discipline, rules and regulations which are aimed to regulate a large number of youngsters. Whereas most Corporates operate with processes and procedures which are aimed at ensuring optimum efficiency and productivity. Moving from an academic environment to a Corporate scenario has many changes and one needs to understand the organisational dynamics in order to get well in this new environment. It could start from simple things like dressing style to serious discipline issues like delivering as promised.

The first thing one needs to learn is that every organisation has its own unique group dynamics. Understanding these dynamics is essential to be able to function efficiently as otherwise a person would end up wasting time and not being able to complete his tasks. In this context there is a concept called extra-constitutional role and power. What this means is that there will always exist a set of people in any organisation who have the ability to influence things in that organisation disproportionate to their stated role and designation. A secretary might be a long time employee and as such enjoys very high credibility and trust with the senior executives. If one were to overlook or look down upon this secretary, the message this person will carry to the senior executives will obviously not be very flattering.

Similarly, there might be a junior level person who knows and understands the various systems and processes of the organisation and more importantly the shortcuts. Identify such people and developing a good rapport with them will obviously help to get things done faster. I know of instances where the trainees were snooty with the security staff and when they had to stay back very late to prepare the project reports the security did not cooperate. Similarly, I also know of individuals who have taken the trouble to build a good rapport with people having extra-constitutional say in the organisation and they are able to get things done faster and easily.

One important point is to keep in mind that this learning about organisational dynamics and operating styles is not only important with regard to the organisation where one works but also with regard to their business partners. A marketing colleague of mine once had to print some special last minute offer coupons. This was decided suddenly and had to be actioned by 1.00 a.m. to be printed and ready for distribution by 7.00 a.m. the following morning. This colleague had a very good understanding of the printers work process as also had a good rapport with various people working there. Instead of calling the person who handles the account, my colleague directly spoke to the print supervisor and got the coupons printed in time.

Lastly learning about the organisation, its working styles, processes, etc., helps any new entrant to settle down fast and start delivering. And obviously anyone who is seen as being able to deliver gets noticed and rewarded.

Personal effectiveness

This is nothing but learning to apply various life skills in the right context and in the right manner. The best example I can give in this context is with regard to coping with stress. There are several books and articles about how to beat stress and how to cope with stress. However, all these books and articles are completely worthless if you start sweating, get anxious and worked up when facing a stressful situation. Instead if various inputs and learning about managing stress are applied, the world will actually become a lot less stressful. So, the next level of learning that needs to fill in the 1st Bucket is applying the life skills to become more effective as a person.

The 1st Bucket for anyone will get filled completely only if you learn, practise, fine tune and repeat the learning cycle again and again. When we are all born, we don't know many things. Most of what we do is based on the concept of habit. Habit is an outcome of learning which can also be defined as repetitive reinforcement. A dancer cannot afford to think every step while giving a performance and similar is the case with most of the things. Repetitive reinforcement internalises these life skills till they become a part of the person and then the response to any situation is more effective.

THE 1ST BUCKET

In short anything new and unknown needs to be explored and learnt in depth. The focus being on the width and depth of learning which then helps translate the information gained into knowledge.

Just imagine the scope of how much of learning is required to fill the 1st Bucket. To do so properly would take a minimum of a few years, because these skills are learnt through experience and repetitions and not by merely reading through a book. Of course there is bound to be scepticism as to whether such simple things require so much of time.

To prove my point I request you to try this exercise. Hold out your hands straight ahead. Move the right hand up and down while moving the left hand from right to left. Simply move one hand vertically while moving the other horizontally. Do this fast and you will realise that such a simple task is not so simple after all. You will be able to do this well enough with some practise which takes time. That is why the 1st bucket needs investment of time as much as effort and cannot be rushed.

> Concentration, Focus and Hand on experience is severely underestimated and an educational qualification alone cannot be a substitute to this.

During this period one should not be distracted by designations, the compensation earned by him as compared to his friends and peers, perks, etc. All these are a natural outcome and will come by default. The single-minded focus has to be on learning and nothing else.

Let me share this story to illustrate the point and highlight how important this single-minded focus is. Many years ago when students would go to Gurukul and stay with the Guru to learn, one youngster started his journey of learning. After many years of hard work, studies and learning the Guru declared that the student had learned all that could be taught and his period of study had come to an end. On the last day of the student's stay in the Gurukul, while having lunch, the student noticed a peculiar smell and very bitter taste in the food being served. As the Guru's wife was considered as one's own mother, the student was hesitating to point out the problem. However, she noticed that something was amiss and asked him about that. He mentioned that something was not right with the food. The Guru then smiled and said that from the very first day castor oil was mixed in his food but he didn't notice that. On when his single-minded focus on learning was over did he notice this. This was in a way a test by the Guru to check where the focus and attention of the students were. But, look at it from the student's point of view. Imagine the depth of his learning if his single-minded concentration was on learning to such an extent that he did not even register the taste of the food eaten.

I am sure that if anyone tried doing this today, there would be an outcry and possibly even a strike.

However, this story drives home the point about learning and how one should not get distracted with anything other than learning during the 1st bucket phase of one's career.

The 2nd Bucket

The 2nd bucket is all about building expertise. In the 1st bucket we have seen various ways and steps which help to build competency. These would make a person competent and effective. However, success is not only about doing a job successfully. It is about excelling in what you do and being known for it. The 2nd bucket is where one can work towards the objective of building this expertise and start the journey to become known for it.

During the 2nd Bucket one has the opportunity to become an expert. If there has been extensive learning in the 1st Bucket one would be clear about his strengths and weaknesses as also in a position to judge which of the learnings can be leveraged better for his personal success. Becoming an expert requires one to have extensive and intensive experience in the field of choice, spanning first hand front line experience to overall strategic exposure. This gives one a true perspective and makes one an expert as also brings about a deep rooted maturity with regard to his expertise.

Research has proven that expertise on anything can be gained through 10,000 hours of practise and experience. *Malcolm Gladwell* in his book *Outliers* repeatedly stresses upon the 10,000 hour rule which in turn is based on research conducted by Dr K. Anders Ericsson, a Swedish psychologist.

Before working on becoming an expert you first need to understand what an expert is and also be clear about what you are going to gain expertise in. An expert is someone who is able to perform much better than his peers and more importantly deliver the committed results. The performance of experts might seem effortless and actually make the whole effort appears to be very easy. That is the true result of expertise based on hours and hours of practise.

At this juncture it is natural for you to wonder about talent and what is the correlation between talent and expertise. Talent is an innate orientation and aptitude to any particular thing. When talent is applied to practise, especially conscious and repeated practise it becomes expertise. Else, the talent becomes wasted.

This is the main reason why so many smart and intelligent people don't appear to succeed whereas many others with relatively lesser levels of intelligence become successful. The difference lies in repeated practise and thereby acquiring expertise. The concept of consciously repetitive learning has already been stressed with regard to filling your 1st Bucket. The same is also important for your 2nd Bucket. Excepting, what you will be filling in the 2nd Bucket is very different from the one you fill in the 1st Bucket.

If you repeat the wrong thing, you master the wrong thing. So, before the many hours of repetition and practise you need to understand and internalise what you need to fill the 2nd Bucket with.

The first decision point is regarding your preference of expertise. Many a time people tend to switch back and forth with regard to this. After many years of experience they suddenly realise that they haven't become an expert and then wonder why. The repetition and experience is relevant and valid only if there is a plan and focus to it. Otherwise repetition of the wrong and misguided actions will become a habit and take a person away from success. This is very similar to travelling to any place. One needs to choose the right route and only then they can travel fast on that route. Travelling fast on a wrong route will not only take a person away from the destination but will ensure that the person gets lost.

So in the 2nd Bucket one needs to focus on whichever area they want to become an expert in and put in best effort consistently and repeatedly for it to work. However, as mentioned above the efforts should be put in the right manner and guidelines which enables these efforts to bear fruit.

The key guidelines one needs to follow to fill the 2nd Bucket effectively, efficiently and successfully are as follows:

- Industry Vs Functional expertise: Our education system teaches us about various functional aspects and concepts. However, only a hand on experience teaches us about an industry. Each industry is unique and has its own quirks. Usually most people tend to get fixated with a function in an industry. This might be alright for a very few types of careers but for the majority of careers, this is actually detrimental. The main reason why it is so is because such a narrow exposure tends to limits a person's perspective and the 2nd Bucket for such a person gets filled with only repetitive experiences.

Therefore the first conscious decision that anyone should take in the process of becoming an expert is whether to focus on an industry or a function. Without this clarity if a person puts in effort it is akin to a bull tied to a water-wheel. The bull walks for many hours a day and works hard to turn the well and pull water; however, at the end of the day it has not made any progress.

If the interest and passion lies in a function as is the case with many people, you should fill your 2nd Bucket with hours and hours of in-depth experience with regard to this function. The trick lies in defining what 'in-depth' stands for. In that context, the unsaid prerequisite for expertise is to know every little thing that pertains to the chosen field of expertise. Take for example an actor. A truly great and expert actor cannot be content with only knowing all the nuances of acting in terms of expressions, voice modulation, etc. The expertise is incomplete unless the actor also learns about camera angles, lighting, some facets of direction, editing, etc. Extending this logic to a related field a great apparel designer cannot be content with knowing about the colours and fashion trends alone. They need to know the technicalities of fabric, how it falls and drapes, the various materials used for accessories, etc. In order to be a functional expert you should have experience of that function across industries and more importantly also learn about all the related fields. For example Sales and Marketing (One of the popular career choices) differs widely from FMCG to Retail to Manufacturing to Services. Unless you have gained experience in these varied applications of the function how can one claim to have developed expertise?

Be clear about where to invest your effort. Water flows along the canal. If the canal is directed to a drain, the water will be wasted.

On the other hand if the passion lies in an industry, be it Retail, Banking, Manufacturing, etc., the focus should be on gaining firsthand knowledge and experience of various functions in that industry. Many youngsters who study management courses aspire to get into strategic decision making roles at the earliest. How can they expect to make sound and valid decisions if they don't have a detailed exposure to various facets of the respective industry? Is this not similar to someone wanting to do open heart surgery immediately after studying MBBS? Even after studying a specialised course a Doctor ventures to do complicated surgery only after having been an understudy of senior doctors. In fact, medicine is probably one of the few professional streams which have adopted this theory by default. One spends years studying the basics and then they study the specialisation. Then they have to undergo practical experience as residents and finally after many years of learning they start being known as an expert or specialist. In this same example, can a Doctor claim to not know anything about giving an injection or starting an IV because that is usually done by a nurse?

So, the first decision point is whether you want to become an expert in a function or an industry. For those who have been working for a while and have already invested time and effort in your career, this is still relevant. You just need to look back and determine the area where your maximum time and effort has been invested. Balance it with you interest and start building on that.

Once a person is clear about the area of interest and starts investing time and effort in mastering that choice, expertise is a default result. Is that right?

Actually, that is completely wrong and misleading. Just as in the case of the 1st Bucket, in the 2nd Bucket also there are several important facets that need attention and conscious development. The absence of these facets will actually nullify the time and effort being invested due to a variety of reasons.

The most important reason for this potential negative effect is the lack of focus and more importantly the lack of some of the important softer aspects required for success. Unfortunately, these softer aspects are hardly ever taught to anyone and most tend to learn it through experience while there are many who go through their careers without realising the importance of these aspects and therefore lose out on the enormous impact these aspects have on a successful career.

It is a common saying in the corporate world that people join and leave good or bad bosses and not an organisation. What is the unsaid implication of this statement?

An expert of an industry or a function need not be a good boss and by extension this expertise does not guarantee good leadership. Whereas it is leadership that actually makes or breaks anyone's career. The next few things that one needs to focus upon during the 2nd Bucket phase and fill the same will help and enable a person to develop into a leader. This coupled with expertise will ensure career success. Both these factors are interlinked. An expert need not be a leader in which case the expertise might become ineffective because there is no team to leverage and use that expertise. Conversely leadership is not only about soft skills and team management as no one wants to follow someone who is floundering about and does not know the subject. Any team member wants to look up to a leader and that involves a level of expertise as a key component of leadership.

Defining your Personal Success Secret

Most leaders are unique. They have their own style and way of doing things. This is in fact a part of the charisma that any leader develops. Nowadays, because of the explosion of information these traits and styles are written about and in many cases touted as a guaranteed way to succeed. No doubt that some of these behavioural patterns are worth emulating and will help anyone become effective and effi cient. But will reading about other successful people and blindly copying them guarantee success? Definitely not.

> Work hard to develop your Personal Success Secret (PSS). There is no substitute for this.

Why is it that an actor is in demand and can demand huge fees while a mimic who copies the actor gets only a fraction of that amount to appear on a few shows and events? It is the difference between originality and copying. No one appreciates a copy, while originality is invaluable.

So the selling of so many self-help, self-development books clearly indicates that many people are looking for a road map to proceed in career and succeed. Contents of most of the books seem to be fresh edited versions of the age old truths or just written differently using new jargon and acronyms. Yet, they sell and many become best-sellers. With so many people reading all these inputs, why is it that success is still elusive and only a few people are able get it?

One reason could be that people read these books, but few bother to practice what is written. But I think there is a majority who do practice and yet seek the next self-help book that comes along. Why is that? Most of these books are pretty simple to follow and written in an easy and understandable manner. Why should it be diffi cult to follow?

This is because successful people have a formula, but there is nothing called as a universal success formula.

OUT OF SYLLABUS

As mentioned earlier a popular actor has worked hard to develop his own style while a mimic only copies that. So, the key lies in developing what I call as "The Personal Success Secret" or PSS in short.

The reason why PSS is crucial and a generic success formula will not work most of the time is because each one of us is unique and we build up varying strengths and have different gaps in our abilities and personalities. Some of us are excellent in planning and leading a structured life, while some cannot function without a chaotic environment. PSS aims at leveraging one's strengths to chart a path to success instead of suggesting that someone copy what someone else did blindly.

I am reminded of the silent film (Oxymoron!) starring Kamal Hassan – 'Pesum Padam' in Tamil and 'Pushpak' in Hindi. In one scene when he is trying to sleep, he just can't fall asleep because he misses the cacophony of his old neighbourhood. So, he makes a recording of the same and plays it to fall asleep. Imagine if he were to instead pick up a book titled "How to fall asleep – Guaranteed to put you to sleep!" – What would have happened?

The book might have suggested all the usual things like avoid coffee or a caffeine closer to bed time, have a cup of warm milk, etc., etc. I am positive, that the book would not have a chapter that deals with recording your neighbourhood sounds which included barking dogs and playing it back to fall asleep!

We are individuals made up of millions of components like looks, voice, height, education, etc. Our personality is a sum total of all these elements and therefore to leverage our personality to pursue success requires a very deep understanding of our constituent factors and the role each plays.

No doubt many self-help books help by indicating the possible action points to aid in a person's development and success. However, for it to work, one needs to first understand oneself completely. Otherwise it would be like giving a map marked in Greek to someone who knows only English. One would feel that he knows where he is heading, but in reality would be completely lost.

The key steps for developing one's PSS –

1. List down all instances of achievements and success. It could be something small like wrangling an extra free item at a store or a major achievement. Such 'wins' are possible only because of certain unique behavioural patterns unique to each one of us. We all have success behaviours and traits and most of the time we are not aware of this. So, the first step is to identify these and the best way to do so is to identify your "wins" and then understand the factors that helped you in that context. Such winning behaviours and traits are there within all of us and are unique to everyone. However, most of us are oblivious to its potential and power in helping create one's PSS and the lack of this self-awareness is itself one of the biggest obstacles to personal success.

2. Consciously make a list of all the elements that went into the making of this 'win' in terms of effort, timing, your interactions, the reactions, how the reactions were managed, etc. Only when all these are consciously thought about

and analysed will the common factor that helps you in such "wins" will emerge and you will become aware of the same.

3. Once you have these common threads and patterns in all these instances of 'winning' start looking at which of these are being repeated by you knowingly and which is being done unknowingly. This is a very important step as this will help you start formalising all those 'winning' behaviours and traits which you are doing unconsciously and therefore can be improved for better impact and effectiveness. Let me share an example. A person who has grown up in a social scenario where they have been taught to participate in the household work and are comfortable doing this will unconsciously offer to help and do any small chore at even a guest's home. This might be a very simple thing. But when contrasted with others who don't do this, such actions become 'winning' behaviour. This will make others appreciate you and think of you in a positive light. If you have analysed and found that this simple and yet unconscious behaviour is actually a 'winning' behaviour for you, it can become a part of your PSS.

4. Lastly, validate this by repeating the first 2 steps for all those times when things did not go well or you were unsuccessful. Just as one should identify 'winning' factors, they should also be aware of the factors that affect them in a negative way. Just as how 'winning' behaviours needs to be identified and consciously repeated

THE 2ND BUCKET

till it becomes a habit, negative factors should be consciously avoided till they disappear from your behaviour patterns and traits. A simple example is regarding smiling. Most of us are not taught to smile consciously. If you notice around you, very few people will be smiling. Smiling, even while on phone can make a huge difference because people can hear the smile in the other person's voice. As an experiment do the following.

☆ Smile consciously from the morning till the night and keep track of how many people smile back at you and how things appear easier and better. The next day, consciously keep a stern face and DO NOT smile the whole day. You will be amazed at the difference you experience between these two days.

Once a person recognises that the lack of smiling is a negative factors and works consciously to develop a smiling habit, automatically their PSS becomes more powerful and effective.

This exercise of identifying and making you aware of the uniqueness that you bring to the table is at the core of creating your PSS. As mentioned just now, it could something as simple as a smile or a sincere look. Maybe when you smile, your face transforms and communicates something powerful. This also clearly makes you aware of your strengths and more importantly your gaps or weaknesses. Work on building your strengths and minimising your weaknesses and you will soon have your PSS and start seeing it in action.

It is actually more important to be aware about your weaknesses because that will enable you to avoid situations where your weakness might become a major obstacle. It is said that efforts to make a fish swim better is far more useful and productive than to complain that they can't fly and try to teach them to fly. This very clearly illustrates the point about focussing on one's strength while being aware about their gaps and weaknesses.

Once a person has this insight and knowledge about himself, then, applying self-help action points becomes easier. And more importantly you will start to keep some action points that enhance your uniqueness and drop the rest. Soon thereafter, emerge the PSS.

People who are already aware of this and scripting their success formulas also read self-help books – in fact, several of them. It is just that they don't blindly try to follow the same. They pick and choose from each and craft their own PSS.

Lastly, one should never try passing on a PSS to anyone, even one's own children because most probably it might not work. Like I said, every successful person has a formula, but there are no universal success formulas.

The role of a Guru or Mentor during this phase is very, very important. Only a good Guru or Mentor would be able to hold a mirror to your face and make your realise not only your potential but also point out the gaps and weaknesses. It is quite easy to mistake any well-wisher as a Mentor and start following his guidance blindly. If the Mentor is not true to being a good Mentor and Guru, it will be worse than having no one to guide or mentor you. The best way to identify a true Guru or Mentor is through two simple acts. First, they will push you to learn and excel and will not spoonfeed you. Second and more importantly they will play on your strengths and will not try to make a fish fly.

Developing Behaviours for Success

We all are taught so many things but some of the most crucial things are never taught to us. Some people stumble, make mistakes and learn from them, while many do not even learn after this. It is said that a Wise man learns from other's mistakes, an Intelligent man from his own mistakes and a Fool never learns from any mistakes.

What if I share with you some of these learnings that successful people have internalised and which is an important reason behind their success? Will that not help you tremendously?

Of course it will help you if you internalise these learnings, act upon them, consciously repeat the same and therefore build it into your positive behaviour through repetitive learning. These are what I refer to as Behaviours for Success. These behavioural patterns when established will become very strong guiding principles in your life and help you achieve success. These are very similar to a light house. The constant beam from a light house guides the ship safely. As mentioned earlier, these are not taught to most of us and therefore the vast majority of people are handicapped by not knowing how to act on these inputs.

These behaviours need to be very consciously developed and nurtured through repetitive learning till it becomes a part of your psyche. As is the case with the most important things in life, they are not complicated and neither are they difficult. These behavioural traits are simple and just needs constant repetition without fail. The four key behaviours for Success are as follows:

OUT OF SYLLABUS

Harmony and Balance

Balance is crucial for anything and everything in life. Human beings are able to walk on two feet and be balanced largely thanks to a small and simple balancing device in our body called inner ear. Most people are not even aware of this fact. Even when sleeping balance is important. I am sure you would have experience an ache in some part of your body at least once because you slept in an awkward position and the body weight had not been distributed properly.

Balance and therefore harmony is an integral part of basic living. Without these two elements, life gets thrown out of gear. Just like how anyone will lose control of a vehicle without balance and get into an accident, a person's life without balance is sure to end up having accidents. You will also agree that being unbalanced and out of control is not the way to achieve success.

> In all the years of technological advancements, no one has been able to improve upon the round shape of a wheel. A well-rounded wheel is the basic need for smooth running and stability. This extends to our life also. The Wheel of Life when balanced ensures Harmony and Success.

More importantly success in one facet of your life becomes meaningless if you are not happy due to some other factors in life. A simple example is the lack of pleasure you might have even after purchasing a very expensive car you wish to purchase if you have neglected your health and have a very bad backache.

The Wheel of Life is a simple training tool commonly used in various training and coaching programs. Unfortunately, this is not internalised and practised properly even by people who attend such programs. The concept of this toll is very simple and is based on identifying the areas of improvement in one's life. Only when you identify the improvement gaps you can work on them to become better.

First draw a circle and four lines and having a rating scale of 0 to 10, as shown in the figure below.

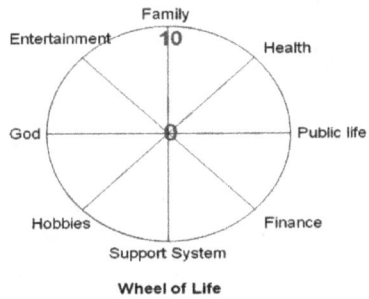

Wheel of Life

You will end up having 8 points of reference which stands for various facets of anyone's life. These can be representatives of any facet of your choice. I have defined it the most commonly applicable aspects of any person's life. The idea is that each of these aspects plays a critical role in the sense of balance and harmony for anyone.

Next rate each of these facets of your life in a realistic manner in terms of how satisfying/ successful you feel that aspect is as of now. For example you might feel that your public life which could be your career or even your studies if you are a student is very good and would rate 8 out of 10. Whereas your support system in terms of friends, relatives, well-wishers, etc., is not too good as you are in a new city and would rate only 4 out of 10. Mark these ratings on the relevant line with a dot.

Once you finish doing this rating for all the 8 facets, join the dots and you will get an uneven wheel. It is extremely rare and even impossible to get an even, round wheel simply because no one's life is perfect.

Very clearly the facets where the wheel is dipping and therefore causing the wheel to be uneven are your gaps or areas for improvement in order to achieve balance and harmony.

If you reflect on why this wheel is uneven, it will usually be due to a disproportionate allocation of time, effort or money towards a few facets as compared to others.

For example, if your health is unsatisfactory you need to reallocate your time, effort and money from some other facet like public life or entertainment towards the facet of health to improve the same. In most of my training programs the participants highlight health as an area of improvement and when there is a discussion it becomes obvious that they are working hard, come back home and finish the home related chores and then to relax watch TV or browse the internet. Before they can realise it, it is very late in the night and they sleep very little as a consequence and therefore wake up feeling tired and irritable. The next day is again a repeat of the same allocation of time and effort and soon the health suffers in terms of dark rings under the eyes, acidity, stress, etc.

Lastly a word of caution; don't expect to balance your wheel of life overnight. It takes months and even years to find the balance in your Wheel of Life because our life situation keeps changing and the demand on our time, effort and money therefore also changes. Be patient and keep working at this and slowly you will perceive balance and harmony emerging in your life which energises you and helps you achieve holistic success. Because of the constant change as mentioned, this exercise needs to be done frequently. It is not something that is done once in a lifetime and forgotten.

This is an important element to fill in your 2nd Bucket because without balance and harmony your efforts are bound to be distracted and when one is distracted and lacks focus, becoming an expert is very unlikely.

Urgent Vs Important

The way you invest your Time, Effort and Money defines your balance as discussed earlier and therefore defines the path to holistic success. If it is so basic and simple, why do so many people fail in doing this properly?

The reality is that they fail because no one teaches us an another important thing in our life. This important thing is the difference between Urgent Vs Important and how to handle the same.

The most common thing for people is to confuse an urgent thing as being important and rush to get it done. This might not be the case and therefore that person is investing time, effort and maybe even money in the wrong thing. This conditioning is due to our upbringing where elders like parents, teachers, etc., define what needs to be

OUT OF SYLLABUS

done by us as priority. You all would have heard, perhaps come across in our life, statements like "I know and I am telling you to do this first". While this may be relevant when we are all young and do not have the capability to judge between urgent and important, it cannot be a constant and permanent orientation. Unfortunately, most people do not get inputs to correct this orientation and they go through life reacting to urgent things.

The lack of clarity about urgent vs important is a trap and leads to an addictive behaviour of responding to urgency most of the time. This orientation is completely useless and unproductive.

Let me share this little secret regarding this.

Urgency is an emotion. The online MacMillan dictionary defines it as "the feeling of wanting something very much or wanting it immediately". It can also be called as a pressure of necessity. But, is it usually a necessity?

Urgency in most cases is externally driven and is a state of mind created by demands, pressures, timelines, etc. I am not saying that there is nothing called as urgent or that it is a mirage. When one is choking or someone is experiencing a heart attack, there can be no mistake, remedial measures are urgently required. However, in most cases, the urgency one experiences or sees an another person going through is externally induced and can definitely be handled better than just reacting blindly or in haste.

Importance on the other hand is an underlying fact. Usually it is long term and requires much thought and lot of effort to accomplish an important task or achievement.

THE 2ND BUCKET

	Low ———— IMPORTANCE ———— High	
High URGENCY	**Priority 4** Interruptions; Some of the Calls, Mails, Visitors, etc.	**Priority 1** Crisis, Fire fighting, Deadline based, etc.
Low	**Least Priority** Time Wasters; Chat – Phone/ Net, etc.	**Priority 2** Proactive, Planning, Strategy, etc.

In order to understand this difference better, look at the diagram below and think of situations from your life which are relevant for each of these boxes.

The High Importance and Low Urgency box is where most expertise is built. Next it is built when doing the High Importance and High Urgency work. Simply because the importance factor ensures that the experience gained in doing that work becomes extremely relevant and a strong foundation for one's career growth and success.

As mentioned before, most of us are unfortunately conditioned to react to only the urgency factor. This is especially true for the urgent but not important tasks because there is usually some amount of external pressure to finish those tasks. The trick lies in learning how to manage that pressure to either reschedule these tasks or minimise the time taken to finish them.

An obvious example is one's health. We all know that health is important and it is the bedrock of almost everything we do in life. Yet, the urgency of several external factors tends to make us neglect and ignore this important thing till it becomes a problem and turns into being urgent as well as important.

Unfortunately most of us are never taught to understand this concept and apply appropriate responses. Therefore, our responses are usually prioritised based on external stimuli and therefore urgent things usually take front seat while some important things tend to get ignored till they either lose their relevance or become urgent and also important.

Time is a wonderful thing. We always value it when there is little or when it is gone. Learn to value it when it is adequate and fill it in the best possible way.

Let me share an another example to explain this point. Suppose you are involved with a senior colleague of yours to prepare a business plan and are finding it of great interest and learning. You know that this is important and that you are being exposed to several things which are making you understand the function and the industry in greater depth. Just when an important part of the plan is being discussed your boss calls for you and tells you to handle an urgent call from a customer who is a very important client. This is not very important but because the customer is waiting for the call it is urgent. One way to handle this situation is to get caught up in the urgency being communicated by your boss and get caught up in the call. The other way to do this might be to call the customer, introduce yourself and diplomatically suggest that you would prefer to meet them as they are VIP clients and schedule an appointment for later. In the second option you have handled the urgent matter quickly without losing time over it and can get back to the important task you are interested in.

Like most of the tools and tips being mentioned in this book, this orientation of thinking and correctly prioritising urgent Vs important tasks does not happen by itself. It is a habit acquired through repetitive learning.

This is an important factor that needs to go into your 2nd Bucket simply because it defines how you allocate time and energy. If you learn this well and start investing time and energy towards experiences that add to your expertise, the objective of the 2nd Bucket is met. Else, you will end up investing your time and effort and at the end of the day will have very little to show for it.

Last but not the least is to consciously be aware of time wasters and avoid them like the plague. It could be things you like doing like browsing on the net with no purpose or have long winded conversations with friends. It might be great fun and pleasurable to indulge in such things, but it does not contribute to your plans to be successful. I am sure that most people with work experience have sat through meetings which seem to go on and on, where the same thing gets discussed again and again. Such time wasters will create habits which are not productive and will actually negate your chances of being successful. In fact, many leading organisations discourage long meetings and some even don't have chairs in meeting rooms. This ensures that people focus on the points of discussion, finish the same and get back to work.

If you do not internalise this and fill your 2nd Bucket with this orientation (wasting time) to make it into a habit, you run the risk of being always busy without any purpose. A real life example is when one sees people rushing to stand up and get their bags in an aircraft which has just landed. Everyone jumps up, pulls out their bags and switches on the mobiles. They impatiently wait for the ladder or aero bridge and rush out. The funny thing is that most of these people in a hurry would be then found waiting for their baggage inside the airport.

Does this false sense of urgency help at all?

Such orientation is more a reflection of a jumbled thought process and every new thought, memory jogged, stimuli received is enough to activate a fresh new frenzy of action. Obviously focus and the right judgement to evaluate urgent Vs important is totally absent.

The point is you should not end up becoming a victim of this and therefore should focus on developing the right orientation with regard to urgent Vs important.

How is it relevant?
I often use the phrase "How is it relevant?" and some of my friends even tease me that my pseudonym is "How is it relevant". I use this phrase very often not because it is a mannerism but to help focus my mind with regard to the situation and the emotional and subconscious response

THE 2ND BUCKET

that invariably is ready to burst forth. This perspective of looking at the relevance of any situation helps redefine the situation and put it in the proper context. Needles to say this then allows me to choose a more appropriate response which is more likely to result in a positive outcome instead of just reacting. Let me share this secret with you as this is a great tool to redefine our focus and perspective.

If we lose perspective and react to a situation, the chances of our getting emotional about it and even carried away is very high. As you know any emotional response is usually very volatile and is guaranteed to get an equally emotional reaction. The important thing to remember is that the reaction need not be always positive. In such a case your energy gets wasted in handling a negative situation and its resultant fall out which includes a bad mood, stress and a complete waste of time and energy.

Remember, during your 2nd Bucket your focus should be on maximising your time spent on the important tasks that increases your experience levels in your chosen area and enhances the chances of your becoming an expert. Anything that distracts you from this focus is a waste of time. "How is it relevant?" is most relevant in that context and should be practised continuously till it becomes a habit.

Let us consider the following scenarios to help understand the application of the "How is this relevant?" thinking:

- ✯ Scene 1: The boss is shouting at a person for no valid reason and the person is miserable.
- ✯ Scene 2: The boss is miserable because the subordinate is not delivering.

OUT OF SYLLABUS

- ★ Scene 3: The entrepreneur is spending a sleepless night because of tough calls required that would impact everyone's life negatively in the short term.
- ★ Scene 4: A friend or a partner fights with you for no reason and one wonders what happened?

The normal human instinct and reaction is to lash out and let loose the anger and frustration that such situations obviously generate in anyone's mind. It is quite natural for anyone in such situation to feel alone, bereft and angry. As mentioned before, this will in return elicit an another round of negative reactions and the net outcome would be a mood filled with negative thoughts and emotions as also a complete absence of focus towards anything other than these thoughts and emotions.

It is at this juncture that one needs to remember the "How is it relevant?" thinking approach. Let's replay the scenes with the 'How is it relevant?' thinking.

- ★ Scene 1: "Your boss is shouting at you for no valid reason and obviously you are miserable". When you ask yourself "How is it Relevant?", you might realise that the boss has been a great enabler in the past and will be so again. So, how is it relevant that he is angry now? Or, the boss has been an insecure and poor leader and anyways, you are looking out for a job, so how is it relevant if he is shouting at you? Anyways, nowadays, most people don't spend their lives in a single job and definitely not with a single boss. So, how is it relevant that someone is shouting at you for no valid reason?
- ★ Scene 2. "You as a boss are miserable because the subordinate is not delivering". You have had several subordinates and will have many more. If

the subordinate does not deliver, move on. How is it relevant? A leader needs to do their best to get the team to deliver and grow. However, if the team is following Murphy's Law of having risen to the heights of their incompetence, what can an individual do? How is it relevant? In this example, I would like to caution about treating the "How is it relevant?" thinking as an excuse for not putting in the best efforts possible by you. However, if there is a situation in spite of the best of efforts, it is better to be dispassionate and move on.

⭐ Scene 3. "The entrepreneur is spending a sleepless night because of tough calls required that would impact everyone's life negatively in the short term". Either the promoter has focussed on the welfare of people before or not. If the welfare has not been the focus, the tough call is a confirmation of the promoter's selfishness, else it's a reaffirmation of the promoter's focus on the overall good and growth of the team and organisation. Sleepless nights; How is it relevant?

⭐ Scene 4. "A friend or a partner fights with you for no reason and one wonders what happened?" Like the promoter example, there have been great times before or not. If there exists memories of great times, then how is the fight relevant? If not and you are going to move on, again how is the fight relevant?

Every event in our life is but a turning point. The fork we choose is based on what has happened before as also the fact that nothing is permanent.

So, getting too involved in the present and getting too involved, especially negatively is just not worth the time and effort. Ask someone who has lived long enough and most situations in life would evoke a memory of having handled it by saying "How is it relevant?".

A word of caution again; this thinking is not an excuse or substitute for relevant and meaningful effort to the best of your capabilities. If you start using this as an excuse to avoid what is to be done by you, only you will suffer. At this point it is relevant to share an interesting story about a teacher and a student.

A teacher was pointing out the North Star and an aleck student decided to have some fun at the teacher's expense. The student pointed to the teacher's finger and said, "That is not a star, sir". The teacher smiled and said, "The North Star has guided generations of mankind and if you cannot see beyond my finger, no one can guide you."

The reason why I am stressing on the misuse of this thinking is that the temptation to do so will be great. It is the easiest thing to walk away from an important but challenging task saying "How is it relevant?". This will definitely hurt you in the immediate, medium and long term course and then the human mind will again try to blame something else and this thinking will be a convenient hook to hang your problems on.

Learning never stops
The 1st Bucket was all about learning. However, learning does not stop with the 1st Bucket alone. The focus during the 2nd Bucket might be building expertise but

an important element of that is that learning continues. Simply because there are newer and newer things that you will discover in your quest for expertise and all these needs to be learnt and mastered. The obvious learning is what one is exposed to in the course of their respective job or work. However, the learning I refer to now is not that kind of learning. It is the ancillary or related learning that is constantly required in one's life. The learning could be about functional topics, Industry related, Soft skills, New technologies and maybe even new hobbies and interests to balance your wheel of life.

Just one golden rule; learning should never stop. Hence consciously seek out things to learn and master.

Let me share a few real life examples.

A great doctor who is an expert surgeon and well known for the success of surgeries cannot afford to become complacent and say that there is nothing else left to learn. So many things are changing starting from the simple but very important sutures; from horsehair to the current self-absorbing types. Technological advances in terms of equipments and procedures. Today one has robotic surgery which requires a very different level of learning. Obviously the great and expert doctor would have to constantly learn and be up-to-date in order to continue being an expert.

Take another example of a very good and capable business leader. Suddenly in the period 2005 to 2010, there was an explosion of various business aids and tools like video conferencing, blackberry, instant messaging, etc. This business leader might have enormous experience and expertise in the chosen field but to remain effective and efficient learning of all these new business tools becomes a must. I personally know a senior manager who used to dictate Emails to a secretary because he was unable to adapt and learn to handle sending and receiving emails. Needless to say, his efficiency and productivity soon declined.

Social media marketing is a fairly recent phenomenon and most marketing experts are still grappling with this, because of which the emerging experts are the younger generation. This is not because this is complicated or difficult. This is just an example of people not keeping their ear to the ground and constantly learning.

Depending on your chosen function or industry the rate of change can vary. But, changes will keep happening and that is guaranteed. Unless you develop an attitude of conscious learning and therefore keep updating and even upgrading your knowledge and skills, the experience and expertise being gained by you in the 2nd Bucket will soon be outdated and not relevant.

It is heartening to see many people who nowadays opting for a management degree after a few years of work experience. This is ideal and in line with the learning orientation of the 2nd Bucket as the conceptual inputs from a good program would help strengthen and focus their learning from the work experience.

To summarise, the 2nd Bucket is all about gaining experience and get on to the path of becoming an expert. The learning and experiences with regard to the function and/ or industry is quite obvious and is also available in several other forums and reference materials.

However all that would become ineffective if you did not focus on the tools, techniques and thinking that has been discussed as part of the 2nd Bucket. Once you internalise these and it becomes a part of your nature and a habit, your focus will be better. A better focus means more concentrated effort which is bound to give you positive results. So remember to fill your 2nd Bucket with all the tools and thoughts mentioned in this chapter and take advantage of the same.

An obvious question in your mind if you are a reader who is midway in your career would be, "How is it relevant to me?".

It is extremely relevant because most of what has been discussed in this chapter and the book is not consciously taught to us. As such a few people get such inputs depending on whether they get a good Guru or Mentor in life and become successful. The others end up wondering about the success of such people.

If you belong to the group of people who have not been taught these things, these new inputs can help you start on your path to success immediately. Most probably you might even know a few things based on your personal experience and learning. However, the trick is to apply all these factors and not only a few of them.

The 3rd Bucket

The 3rd Bucket is actually the most difficult and needs tremendous care and attention to fill. This is mainly because of the fact that there will be many people looking up to you or looking closely at what you do when you are in the life stage when the 3rd Bucket typically comes up.

If you have filled the 1st Bucket with loads of learning and your 2nd Bucket with lots of experience and expertise while balancing your life, continuous learning and juggling between the important and urgent things, there is only one thing you need to fill your 3rd Bucket with; Recognition and the Rewards associated with it.

The 3rd Bucket is when people respect you for the professional you have become and value your expertise. Organisations want to tap into your expertise to benefit from the same, others want to work with you to learn from you and in short, you are in demand.

Is that not a very nice and even heady feeling?

But this will not happen by itself. You need to work towards developing your personal branding consciously by sharing your expertise in public forums and be known for your expertise. When this is done properly all kinds of success follows you by default.

However, the 3rd Bucket also needs some filling to be done apart from the development of personal branding. Personal branding works best when others start to speak about you and your expertise. Apart from promoting yourself in various ways, one needs to fill the 3rd bucket with three important things. Each of these is very important and ignoring even one or all of these will lead to imbalance.

Confi dence Vs Overconfi dence

By this time a person would have experienced a variety of situations and scenarios, handled different kinds of people, made mistakes and hopefully learn from them and of course be confident of their skills, abilities and competencies. At the same time there exists a risk of this confidence exceeding the real level of competence and abilities and ends up being overconfidence.

A simple explanation about confidence Vs overconfidence is if you were to think that you can jump 10 feet high, that is confidence. It could actually motivate you to put in your best efforts to jump that high or even higher.

However if you feel that **only you** can jump 10 feet high, that is overconfidence. This kind of thinking is typically a result of what is known as a superiority complex

> Some of the most successful companies are already finalising a newer model when launching a new product. This is because they know that the world is full of equally smart people.

or attitude. When a person starts to think that he is better than all the others and no one else can equal him, it leads to a feeling of being overconfident.

If you recall, one of the important things to fill in your 1st Bucket is life skills and self-awareness is one of these skills. True self-awareness comes only when one has a realistic sense of his capabilities. If a person were to overestimate his capability or underestimate the capabilities of others it would be a serious mistake.

History has several examples of great leaders and extremely smart people who failed more due to over-confidence than anything else. Most strategy books including the famous "The Art of Warfare" by Sun Tzu talks about this point relating to a realistic assessment of self and others.

An interesting translation of the verse from this book's third chapter is as follows:

- "If you know the enemy and know yourself, you need not fear the result of a hundred battles.
- If you know yourself but not the enemy, for every victory gained you will also suffer a defeat.
- If you know neither the enemy nor yourself, you will succumb in every battle."

Overconfidence invariably is a manifestation of the second and third statement. When a person thinks too highly about his capabilities and underestimates others, he neither knows himself nor others and success is definitely not possible.

So the key learning during the 3rd bucket is developing a balanced mind which has a realistic perspective of one's strength and weaknesses and more importantly acknowledges the same in others. The challenge will be to develop this mind-set and maintain this in a situation where people are praising you and talking about your achievements, sometimes in an exaggerated manner. In order to fill your 3rd Bucket properly and move ahead successfully, this orientation of self-confidence is essential and equally important is the need to avoid becoming overconfident.

What is the "Wallenda Factor" and how to avoid it

This is a fairly uncommon term and it would be better to explain what the "Wallenda factor" is all about. This refers to the fear of falling or failing. Shortly after Karl Wallenda who was a famous aerialist fell to his death in 1978 (traversing a 75-foot high wire in downtown San Juan, Puerto Rico), his wife, also an aerialist, discussed that fateful San Juan walk, "perhaps his most dangerous." She recalled: "All Karl thought about for three straight months prior to it was falling. It was the first time he'd ever thought about that, and it seemed to me that he put all his energies into not falling rather than walking the tightrope." An aerialist is an acrobat who performs in the air and the art is very dangerous even when safety apparatus is being used. So, the state of mind is very important while performing.

Mrs. Wallenda added that her husband even went so far as to personally supervise the installation of the tightrope, making certain that the guide wires were secure, something he had never thought of doing before. When Karl Wallenda poured his energies into not falling rather than walking the tightrope, he was virtually destined to fall.

Most people and even organisations tend to develop this orientation over a period of time, especially when they become more successful. When one starts off life with little to lose, the focus is on trying new things, experimenting, taking risks. The focus is on learning, experiencing and growth. Usually this makes life richer, more interesting and lot of fun. One gets caught in a positive cycle which often is self-sustaining.

> Your mind directs its energies on whatever dominates it. Dominate your mind with positivity and the mind will direct its energies to positive outcomes.

For an average person, then comes marriage, children, monetary responsibilities, home loan EMI's and a focus on savings. And along with it comes a shift in focus and orientation. Usually this shift is not balanced or planned well and is the starting of a vicious cycle of stress and unhappiness. This is where the orientation to constantly balance your wheel of life will help.

Slowly the focus is on managing the unknown future, usually through a monetary cushion. This is the crux of the issue. We fear the unknown! In fact that's the single biggest reason why death inspires so much of discomfort and fear. One does not know for sure what lies on the other side.

So, with the change in focus the Wallenda Factor kicks in fully. One gets increasingly bogged down in avoiding failure.

When one is young the focus is on success and usually he succeeds over a period of time. And then the focus shifts on sustaining the success which is positive and good. However, more often than not it actually ends up becoming a focus on avoiding failure. This leads to less of innovation and experimentation and more of reviews and analysis. I remember a comment which aptly describes the latter behaviour; "Driving while looking only in the rear view mirror". Is it any wonder that accidents happen? Such an overcautious approach invariably tends to focus on the mistakes and failures and is what is cautioned against.

Over a period of time, one finds that the conversation centres increasingly around the good old days.

This has been discussed and debated in the leadership context in various publications and not succumbing to the Wallenda Factor is considered to be an important leadership trait and key to sustainable success.

In order to recognise and avoid this orientation, learn to accept things that can't be changed and put in efforts for only those which can be changed. Fearing and working to manage an unknown variable is completely useless and will only create stress.

OUT OF SYLLABUS

Accept that the unknown will always be unknown. Also accept that change is the only constant in life and that life has to have up and down cycles. Whatever goes up comes down and vice versa. In this orientation there is no fear of failure or getting fixated by such a thing. A good example to explain this is about an elderly person who gives his son two boxes and says that they contain a very powerful secret. He instructs his son to open one box when he is in the worst possible problem and there seems to be no solution in sight and the other box when the son is very successful, content and everything is happening as desired.

The elderly person passes away and after a few years the son is faced with a miserable situation where he has many problems and life does not seem worth living. He suddenly remembers his father's advice and takes out the relevant box and opens it. Inside the box is a small piece of paper which says "This will pass and times will change". The son is greatly motivated and puts in greater efforts and soon all the problems are solved and he is very happy.

After a few years he is very content and satisfied with the way life has shaped up. His successes in business and personal life are very satisfying and there is nothing that he can complain about. He suddenly remembers the second box and opens that. Inside the box is a small piece of paper which says "This will pass and times will change". The son realises that just like his previous problems the current situation will also change and therefore it is far better to focus on the good things in the present instead of worrying about what will happen.

The take out from the story is to accept change and not shy away from the occasional failures. More importantly one should not start becoming failure-fixated instead of success-focussed. The key being fixated is negative while focussed is positive orientation.

In short, keep the child inside you alive, well and kicking. Be curious, experiment and enjoy the journey of life. Any child learns and grows because they are not afraid of falling down. Imagine if a child were to think that he has just now started crawling and falling down is a big risk of trying to walk. That child will end up crawling around throughout his life.

People first

There is an absolutely fantastic film about leadership which actually explains the process of how one becomes a leader. The film shows a young man dancing in a park kind of place and is oblivious to others watching him. He is enjoying himself and lost in the music and his dance.

After a short while another person stands up and joins him in the dancing and then a few more. Again for a while this small group of people is dancing and then suddenly many more people realise the fun that this group is having and join the dancing. Very soon, most of the people who are there, are dancing and enjoying themselves.

Most people would say that the young man is a leader and he is the person who has made almost everyone to start dancing. The reality is slightly different. This young man is someone who is enjoying himself. The first few people who have joined him in this dancing as his followers have made him into a leader. They are the ones who have influenced others to overcome their shyness and join the dancing. The fact is that however long the young man has danced, no one would have joined in till they see someone else is also ready to participate. This is a common human trait.

As such the followers, team members, etc., are the people who help to create a leader. Most of the successful leaders know about this fact and therefore value and cherish their team. Is it any wonder that in most leadership training programs the main topic covered pertains to team building and motivation?

As a continuation of the first point, it is very easy to lose sight of the role of followers or team members due to a feeling of overconfidence or even arrogance. It is very easy to get carried away by success and start thinking that the followers or team members have not contributed to one's leadership and success. Nothing can be further from the truth. In the 3rd Bucket, you must consciously learn to value people, especially your team mates and their contribution and support.

Putting people first does not stop with only your team mates and followers. One must learn to genuinely care and show respect for everyone they meet and interact with. During this phase it is quite probable that you are surrounded by people who want to make you feel important for selfish reasons. They will sometimes even act rudely to others just to show to you how important they think you are. One should never get carried away by such people and lose sight of the basic human courtesy and respect.

Great people are known to be great not because of only their success but more so because their success does not make them arrogant, rude or insensitive. The world will always value someone who is respectful and sensitive. Most stories about truly great people involve incidents of how they would wish each employee in the company regardless of their designation or how they would insist on joining the line and waiting for their turn or extending their personal help to someone during a crisis, etc. Essentially they put people first.

There is a concept of leadership which defines them based on Task orientation and People orientation. Task orientation is focussing on the work and task at hand and everything else is secondary. This is good and definitely efficient. However, people might get neglected and therefore motivation might be poor, involvement and commitment might not be there. On the other hand is a people orientation. When people are most important and work is considered secondary, the people feel very nice and are obviously happy. However, the work might suffer. The ideal is an equal focus on task and people where the task is important and people are also given their due importance.

This learning about people first is not about becoming only people orientated and putting tasks as secondary. It is about realising that people have a very important role to play in any facet of a person's life and to give them their due importance. More importantly develop a people orientation which is genuine and a part of your personality simply because a false interest is the first thing noticed by others and is not possible to be sustained.

I would like to quote a simple yet most relevant advice given by the hero of a popular Hindi movie about how to judge whether a person is genuine or not. In the movie he says that observe how a person calls out to others. If makes a sound like "Tsk-tsk" or whistles, it shows a very poor regard for others.

The larger issue is the lack of respect towards an another human being, especially those who are rendering a service. If anyone ends up having this attitude it will be extremely difficult to gain mutual respect and the respect and regard that others show towards you will be because of the designation and power of your position. The day you lose the position and designation, the respect and regard will also go with it.

So, 'people first' is very crucial to ensure that people respect you and look up to you as a person and not for the designation. I will end with a simple and powerful example to drive home the importance of this learning.

I happened to interact with a person who was the head of a large organisation and obviously kept people on his toes. Once he had finished a meeting and came out to take the lift. Whenever this person comes or leaves the office, one staff member has to hold the lift at the appropriate floor for however long it is required. The staff member had changed his hands to hold the door open button after pressing on the same for quite some time. In that split second, someone must have pressed the call button and the lift moved to an another floor. This head of the organisation chose exactly that moment to come and found that he had to wait for the lift. It was rather sad to see the way the staff member was scolded and even humiliated, all because he had not held the lift waiting. Now the funny part is that after some time this head retired and happened to come to the office. Funnily enough, he was kept waiting for the lift because a staff member was holding the lift for the new head of that organisation. Obviously that person's lack of people first thinking affected him since people had been fearful only of his designation and position and did not care about the person per se.

Contrast this with some of the leaders I have worked with. Even after having left the organisation if they were to drop in I have seen people walk out from important meetings to spend time and interact.

That's the difference between respect and regard for a person Vs his designation. A successful person always commands this respect because in turn he always puts people first.

In summary the 3rd Bucket needs to be filled with efforts to build your personal brand while guarding against the pitfalls of overconfidence, arrogance and taking people for granted. Like almost everything else mentioned in the book, this is a result of personal orientation and will neither happen automatically nor overnight. You need to consciously practise this repetitively till it becomes a habit.

The most important one; The 4th Bucket!

Till now I have been talking about what you need to fill your various buckets with. While you have been filling the 1st, 2nd and 3rd Bucket with things for your success and gradually moving towards your success, you would have had many experiences, learnt a great many things and have deep insights and learning about a wide range of subjects.

As mentioned in the section pertaining to developing your PSS a Guru or Mentor plays a very important role in most people's life and their success. But unfortunately very few people get a good Guru or Mentor.

With so many people with wide experiences and expertise in so many fields around, is it not puzzling why only a few people get a good Guru or Mentor?

The problem lies in the potential Guru or Mentor.

Usually with years of experience the chances of one being humble and not taking himself too seriously becomes very remote. So, the majority of people carry around this enormous amount of experience and expertise, also carry lots of ego, self-importance and attitude.

Such people are ready to provide guidance and inputs only if it is followed blindly. Actually, it is not given as an input but more like orders. The fact that one size fits all does not work in life is forgotten. Is it any wonder that finding a good Guru or Mentor is so diffi cult?

Advice and inputs should fall softly like snow. Only then will it seep deep into the minds of the recipient like how snow melts and the water seeps into the ground.

It has been said and also proved in many people's lives that what is given comes back a 100 fold. So give freely and give positive things only.

The 4th Bucket is all about you becoming a good Guru or Mentor.

Till this stage one would have got many things from many people in terms of inputs, support, guidance, encouragement, etc. All these would have helped him in achieving success. It is quite diffi cult to go back and try to reciprocate by trying to give back something to everyone who has contributed to your life.

The best way to do this is to give back to others freely in terms of all the positive things that you have got. In that way you are setting in force a positive cycle which will ensure that many Gurus and Mentors are formed over time and no one suffers from the lack of proper guidance and inputs. However, remember to take on the role of a Guru or Mentor after having shed your ego aside.

THE MOST IMPORTANT ONE; THE 4TH BUCKET!

Your role should be limited to the right path and providing the illumination of knowledge. You should not insist that everything you say is right and everything else is wrong. Because if anyone says that, it is the biggest mistake he can make.

So, what is in it for you? How will this fill your 4th Bucket?

This will actually fill your 4th Bucket with immortality. Is it hard to believe?

Think back and you will readily remember all those people who have helped you (directly or indirectly); a few or more of them might not have done much. However, what they did was meaningful and without ego; this created a positive effect on your life and a permanent memory.

This memory always will bring back a nice and warm feeling along with missing the presence of that person. Is that not immortality?

When people are asked about the inventor of television, most used gadget today. Most of them don't know the answer. Yet, they will fondly remember and talk about people who made a difference to their lives. Is that not immortality?

Ask people about the winner of Nobel Prize for medicine in 1995. You will get blank stares. Yet, they will remember with gratitude people who guided them to win awards and get success. Is that not immortality?

So, the 4th Bucket is all about filling your life with the giving to others by guiding them without any selfishness and with no hidden agendas.

Take the trouble to teach, train, guide, mentor, counsel and advice others, especially the youngsters. In that context remember that your expertise and experience might not lie in this area. For example if you are a successful aeronautical expert, you might not automatically become a great teacher, trainer or mentor.

So, you need to take the trouble to learn the art of teaching, training, mentoring, etc., because they require certain skills. The theme of learning continues in the 4th Bucket as only that will enable you to teach and guide others.

The Last Word

I would like to leave you with a few thoughts if you are to truly benefit from having read this book and the ideas, tools and techniques mentioned in this book.

Firstly, as already mentioned under the 1st Bucket, my personal view is that there is no success formula and everyone needs to develop their own success formula. In that context everything is an input and should not be taken as gospel truth. The formula for success lies in each individual's own hands. As such, this theory is indicative. Take it, craft it, mould it to suit your personality and hopefully you would create your own successful version.

> The day you start to blindly follow something is the day you move away from success. Individuality is the first hallmark of success.

Secondly, the book deals with what I think are some very crucial elements which help a person become successful. There are so many things exist that one needs to learn and master. Obviously not everything can be fitted into one book. As such the repeated message of learning continuously is very important. There is a saying in Tamil which means that whatever one manages to learn is only a handful, while all that is to be learnt is as big as the world itself. As such, take these inputs as stepping stones towards success, which they truly are.

Next is the importance of perseverance. Nothing happens overnight. Take for example the wheel of life. Just because you do that exercise does not mean that everything will become balanced immediately. It will take time and repeated efforts to start seeing significant changes and results. So, the question is how will one remain motivated enough to persevere?

Either they can be motivated by their personal goal or they can look for motivations in small wins. Small wins are small things which start to go right and are rewards for your efforts. Many people tend to ignore these small wins because this is not what they were aspiring for. Many people even get frustrated by small wins because their expectations was for something more. A very few number of people realise that these small wins are like sign posts to indicate that you are on the right path and therefore continue their perseverance of efforts. That is why one sees more people feeling frustrated and stressed while only a few seem to be successful.

The reality is that we are all working towards success. If we recognise and celebrate these small wins, the larger success is only some distance away. Alternatively, if we get frustrated and give up, we end up moving away from success.

Take a simple example. When you are going from one place to an another you are constantly checking the distance by looking at the roadside signs. Or you check the stations that have passed by to know how much further your destination is. Every such station passed is a small win. If one gets frustrated and angry that the station that passed by was not the destination and got down from the train, they will never reach the destination at all.

I have mentioned about the role of a Guru/ Mentor in the book. Such people are crucial in guiding a person on the right path. One word of caution: As also mentioned in the book, be careful of whom you acknowledge as your Guru or Mentor. However, once you have done so, believe in that person and act on their inputs with full faith. More importantly do not try to evaluate and be critical of your Guru or Mentor. No one is perfect. However, the Guru or Mentor has something valuable to offer to you and because of these qualities you have accepted him as your GURU in the first place. After accepting him, if you start analysing and judging him you are only harming yourself.

A simple example for this is the story from the *Mahabharata* where Ekalavya did not question his Guru's intention when his thumb was demanded as a Guru *Dakshina*. Even though the Guru was motivated by a negative thought when asking for such an offering, the complete surrender of Ekalavya to his Guru has ensured that his name is remembered even today. Most people associated with sports and other variety of fields and industries can share examples of how a Mentor has completely turned around lives and put people on the path to success even though the Mentor might not have

OUT OF SYLLABUS

been a very successful person. The lesson to remember is complete faith you should repose on your Guru or Mentor.

Lastly, on the topic of faith; it is the bedrock for everything in life. Today studies are beginning to prove that prayers can actually help heal a sick person faster. The reality is that the power of one's mind is neither understood nor realised by most people. Our minds are such wonderful and capable things which are grossly underutilised. One of the greatest fuels for generating the power of one's mind is faith.

Faith can unleash so much of mental and intellectual potential that one cannot even imagine the same.

If you were to ask anyone about the most important factors that help an army win or lose, the chances are they will talk about the number of soldiers, weapons, bombs, fighter planes, etc. However, the reality of what makes an army win or lose is simply food and fuel. The best of strategy and the most advanced of weapons is a complete waste if the soldiers are faint with hunger and the most modern of equipments fail if they don't have fuel to operate.

In the same way, the most important element of success is one's mental, intellectual and emotional capabilities. These capabilities are unleashed to the maximum when powered by faith.

The obvious question would be why I have written so many pages about all these tools and techniques while I am mentioning about this most powerful factor in the last chapter and in such a brief manner.

It is because, faith cannot be taught. People need to develop it by themselves. The celebration of the small win orientation will help develop faith. However, one needs to have the basic faith in himself and in a superior power that can be called as God, Fate, etc. Without this faith, the effort given will be more and the results will be less. With faith it will be the reverse.

Have a strong faith, use these inputs as guiding stones and develop your own personal success.

Remember the 4th Bucket and share with others your success and secret of your success. What you give comes back to you. Give positive things to get positive things in your life.

All the Best

www.ingramcontent.com/pod-product-compliance
Lightning Source LLC
Chambersburg PA
CBHW070337230426
43663CB00011B/2358